BOUDICCA AND THE ANCIENT BRITONS

Lucilla Watson

Illustrated by Mark Bergin

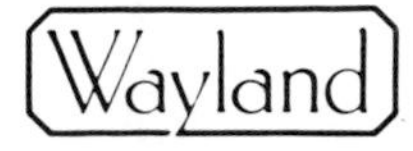

LIFE AND TIMES

Alexander the Great and the Greeks
Boudicca and the Ancient Britons
Cleopatra and the Egyptians
Julius Caesar and the Romans
Alfred the Great and the Saxons
Canute and the Vikings
Confucius and Ancient China
William the Conqueror and the Normans
Chaucer and the Middle Ages
Richard the Lionheart and the Crusades
Columbus and the Age of Exploration
Montezuma and the Aztecs
Elizabeth I and Tudor England
Atahuallpa and the Incas
Oliver Cromwell and the Civil War
Pepys and the Stuarts
Daniel Boone and the American West
Dickens and the Victorians

Further titles are in preparation

First published in 1986 by
Wayland (Publishers) Ltd
61 Western Road, Hove
East Sussex BN3 1JD, England

British Library Cataloguing in Publication Data
Watson, Lucilla
Boudicca and the ancient Britons. — (Life and times)
1. Boadicea, *Queen of the Iceni* — Juvenile literature 2. Great Britain — History — Roman period, 55 BC-AD 449 — Biography
3. Great Britain — Queens — Biography
I. Title II. Bergin, Mark III. Series
936.2'04'0924 DA145.3.B6

ISBN 0 85078 649 5

Phototypeset by Planagraphic Typesetters Ltd
Printed in Italy by G. Canale & C.S.p.A., Turin
Bound in Great Britain at The Bath Press, Avon

Contents

Above *The bronze statue of Boudicca, near the Houses of Parliament in London, is probably not a very good likeness to the real Boudicca.*

1 BOUDICCA AND THE ROMANS

Boudicca

Boudicca is remembered today for her heroic but unsuccessful stand against the Roman forces that had occupied Britain in the middle of the first century AD. Her name means 'Victoria', or 'Victory'. She was 'very tall, the glance of her eye most fierce; her voice harsh. A great mass of the reddest hair fell down to her hips. Around her neck was a large golden necklace, and she always wore a tunic of many colours . . . Her appearance was terrifying.' This description of the power and impressiveness of her physical appearance is taken from one of the few sources of information about her, the records of Roman historians. From these, and from the discoveries of archaeologists, we must build up our picture of Boudicca and the life of the Ancient Britons.

The bronze statue of Boudicca that you can see near the Houses of Parliament in London was erected only about a hundred years ago. It probably bears little likeness to her actual appearance — in fact, if Boudicca could see her statue today, she probably would not recognise herself, or her chariot. This is only because people a hundred years ago knew much less about the Ancient Britons than we do today. The name on the statue — Boadicea — is also wrong; we now know that 'Boudicca' is more accurate.

Right *A triumphant Boudicca holding her shield and bloodied sword.*

An uneasy peace

By the year AD60, the Ancient Britons had suffered Roman rule for just over fifteen years. When the Romans first appeared on their shores, the Ancient Britons had put up fierce and determined resistance to the invading forces. However, the Romans had eventually managed to establish themselves on British soil, and by this time the south and east of the country had been conquered.

The bold, confident Romans treated the defeated Britons harshly, seizing farmland and cattle for their own use and taking women and children to keep as slaves. Important tribal centres were occupied in order to assert Roman power and dominance over the native population. In addition, they built fine, strong cities of their own at Colchester, St Albans and Chelmsford, as well as establishing a busy trading post on the River Thames that would eventually become the city of London. They also began to build roads, one of which, known as Watling Street, stretched from London to St Albans, a distance of 39 kilometres (24 miles).

The Ancient Britons had been ill-equipped to deal with

Above *Under Roman domination, the defeated Britons could only look on as their women and children were led off to become slaves.*

the strength and organization of the Roman army. Some tribes had fallen meekly under Roman rule, but others were angry that their land had been invaded and their way of life upset. As time went on, feelings of discontent and a desire for revenge grew in strength. Although they had to contend with frequent skirmishes and minor rebellions, the Romans were unprepared for the uprising that was about to occur. Nor could they have expected that its leader would be a woman, Boudicca.

Those tribes of Ancient Britons that lived around the area of Colchester had made an uneasy peace with the Romans. Each agreed not to attack the other and, in return for food and hostages, the Romans promised them protection from attacks. One such tribe was the Iceni, whose king, Prasutagus, was the husband of Boudicca.

The beginnings of a revolt

Prasutagus hoped that the fragile peace that he had managed to maintain with the Romans during his lifetime could be continued after his death. However, his wishes were ignored and the Romans seized the chance to attack the Iceni and to remove the royal family from power. The Iceni palace was captured and Boudicca was flogged, along with her daughters.

This was an outrageous act and Boudicca was naturally furious. She persuaded other tribes to join forces with her own armies in an attempt to overthrow the cruel Romans. Their first actions met with great success. They destroyed Colchester, burning its fine buildings, smashing its statues and ransacking its temple. They dealt similarly

with Chelmsford and St Albans before moving on to the Roman port of London. Some Romans managed to escape before the ferocious army arrived. Many others perished, hacked to death or burned in the fierce fires started by the attackers. Having reduced to ruins the proudest achievements of the Romans in Britain, namely the towns of Colchester and London, Boudicca and her army could not pause for long to take stock of the situation. Those Romans who had managed to flee from London were making their way up Watling Street to join their armed forces based further north. In order to claim total victory, Boudicca knew that she must pursue these Romans and prevent them taking their revenge.

Below *Following the flogging of Boudicca and her daughters some tribes of Ancient Britons joined together to try and overthrow the Romans.*

The final battle

Above *Both sides of a Roman copper coin of Antonius Pius which commemorated his victories in Britain.*

It is not known precisely where Boudicca and her army caught up with the Romans on Watling Street. Nor has the location ever been discovered of one of the bitterest and most bloody battles ever fought in England. It may have been near Nuneaton in Warwickshire, on the site of the present-day village of Mancetter, or Manduessedum ('Place of Chariots') as the Romans knew it.

In expectation of the attack, the Romans arranged their army on a narrow piece of land with hills and woods behind them and a river in front. The soldiers of Boudicca's army were gathered on the opposite bank, shouting and banging on their shields to frighten the Romans. The Iceni were confident of victory. Their women, children and old men stood or sat on carts parked in a circle nearby, waiting for the battle to begin.

Boudicca gave the order to charge before the Romans were ready. The Romans were heavily outnumbered by the Ancient Britons, but they had the advantage of better weapons and superior organization. They replied to the advance of the Britons by hurling their javelins into their ranks. They then engaged in hand to hand combat, fighting hard with their short swords. The Roman cavalry quickly surrounded Boudicca's army and crushed it against the circle of carts. Although Boudicca tried to surrender, the Romans were keen to take full revenge for the destruction of their towns. Even the women and children were put to death.

For Boudicca, this was a cruel defeat. She poisoned herself and was buried secretly by those of her faithful tribesmen who had managed to survive the battle.

Left *Boudicca's army was no match for the Roman cavalry.*

2 THE ANCIENT BRITONS

Above *The Aylesford bucket is a good example of Bronze Age craftsmanship.*

Who were the Ancient Britons?

The Ancient Britons were the original inhabitants of present-day England, Wales, Scotland and Ireland. People started to come to Britain from the continent of Europe at the end of the Ice Age, around 8,000 BC. These settlers were simple, nomadic hunters. Then, about 4,000 BC, they were joined by people who introduced primitive farming, rearing animals and growing crops. Then, around 2,000 BC, another wave of settlers arrived, bringing with them knowledge of bronze working. This was the beginning of the Bronze Age and it was during this period that the great monuments of Stonehenge and Avebury were built.

In about 450BC there came the next major movement of people into Britain, arriving in southern England from France and Germany. These people were Celts. They were renowned for their artistic and warlike abilities and, more importantly, skilled in the use of iron. It was their arrival that began the Iron Age in Britain. The last people

Right *This Celtic bronze shield is about 2,000 years old.*

to come to Britain before the Roman invasion were the Belgae, a Celtic tribe from northern France. They settled in south-eastern England and had slightly different habits from the rest of the Ancient Britons.

So, by Boudicca's time, Britain was inhabited by people of mixed origins who had arrived at different times and for different reasons. Some had come because they had been driven out of their original native land. Others had come to raid and had stayed to farm, while some arrived specifically to conquer parts of Britain. All these people are known as Ancient Britons and their language was British. Boudicca lived at the end of the Iron Age, the period that we shall be concentrating on. When the Romans finally conquered Britain, they wiped out the way of life of the Ancient Britons and brought the Iron Age to an end.

Below *Members of a Celtic tribe arriving on the shores of Ancient Britain.*

Above *An Iron Age tribe contained people of many different professions: 1. Servants; 2. Craftsmen; 3. Farmers; 4. Druids; 5. Warriors; 6. Nobles; 7. Tribal king.*

The Ancient Britons in the Iron Age

By the time of the Iron Age, the Ancient Britons were divided into over thirty tribes. These inhabited all parts of Britain, from the tip of Cornwall right up into Scotland and throughout Wales and Ireland (see map on right). The most important of these tribes were the Silures in South Wales, the Ordovices in North Wales, the Dobunni at Bagendon, the Durotriges in Dorset, the Catuvellauni at Wheathampstead, and the Trinovantes in Essex. The Iceni, Boudicca's tribe, occupied part of East Anglia.

Each tribe had its own king, who ruled over his territory from a tribal centre. Cunobelinus, king of the Trinovantes, for example, ruled from a great tribal centre at Colchester. Here, important business was carried out, and people came to buy and sell at the markets.

The tribal king was the most important person in Iron Age society. He was advised by a group of counsellors, consisting of powerful nobles, learned priests and seers, or druids. Below them in rank came the warriors and charioteers, poets and musicians, the finest craftsmen, and the land-owning farmers. The ordinary people in Iron Age society were mostly poor farm-workers and simple craftsmen. These hard-working, modest folk formed the bulk of the population. They enjoyed none of the riches that the king and his nobles took for granted.

But for the rich and poor alike, it was not always a peaceful life. Some tribes were more powerful, greedy and aggressive than others. Consequently battles, raids and skirmishes occurred frequently. In fact, as the Iron Age progressed, tribal hostilities grew and attacks by stronger tribes on weaker ones became more common. To help protect themselves from the threat of such attacks, the Ancient Britons developed elaborate defensive fortifications, such as hillforts.

Below *This map shows where some of the main tribes had settled in Ancient Britain by the time of the invasions of Julius Caesar in 55* BC *and 54* BC.

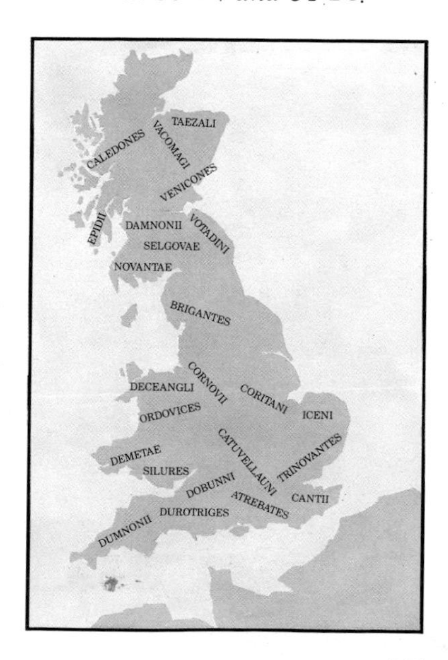

3 DEFENCES AGAINST ATTACK

Building a hillfort

The Ancient Britons put a great deal of effort into building their hillforts. First of all, they chose a suitable hill, or spur of land, which commanded a good view of the surrounding countryside.

Once the hill was chosen, a team of men with spades and shovels began to dig a ditch around the top of the hill, while others loaded the loose earth into baskets. The loose earth was then emptied on the ground above the ditch, so that a steep bank was formed. When the ditch and the bank were finished, carpenters sank dozens of planks into the ground to make a palisade above the ditch. The earth that had been dug out of the ditch was then packed tightly against the inside of the palisade and reinforced with

Below *Maiden Castle was captured by the Romans in the first century AD.*

Above *A hillfort under attack. The most complicated hillforts were constructed with two or even three ditches to foil attackers.*

stones. This formed a rampart, which allowed guards to stand and look out over the palisade.

With a ditch, a bank and a palisade, the simplest form of hillfort was complete. An enemy attacking the fort would be forced down into the ditch, only to be pelted with stones and javelins thrown from the defensive positions on the ramparts above.

Having ensured that the enemy had no hope of getting over the walls, further precautions were taken to fortify the main gate. At first, entrances to hillforts consisted of simple timber gates that were placed across a gap in the ramparts. More advanced versions were cleverly designed to trap the enemy. These entrances were narrow passages that wound backwards and forwards, enabling defending guards to attack the enemy from the ramparts above. These winding entrances are called hornworks.

In addition to these complicated hornworks, some hillforts had two sets of gates. The aim of this might have been to create an isolation chamber, where unexpected or unknown callers could be detained and questioned to determine whether they were friend or foe.

Inside the hillfort

Above *Celtic clay pots were beautifully decorated.*

Some hillforts were only used as places of refuge in times of war, or when danger from marauding tribes threatened. Others were probably occupied all the time, housing several families and supporting a bustling village life. Circular and rectangular huts were used as living quarters. Their walls were made of wattle and daub supported by a wooden framework, with a doorway on one side. Thatch or turf was used to make a roof, through which a hole was made to allow smoke from the hearth to escape.

Hillforts were busy places. Women ground corn, spun wool or wove on upright looms, while their children played beside them. Elsewhere, blacksmiths made iron sickles and cooking implements, or mended armour. There were also pottery works, where jars and bowls were made.

Below *In times of war, farmers, their families and their animals, took refuge within the hillfort's defences.*

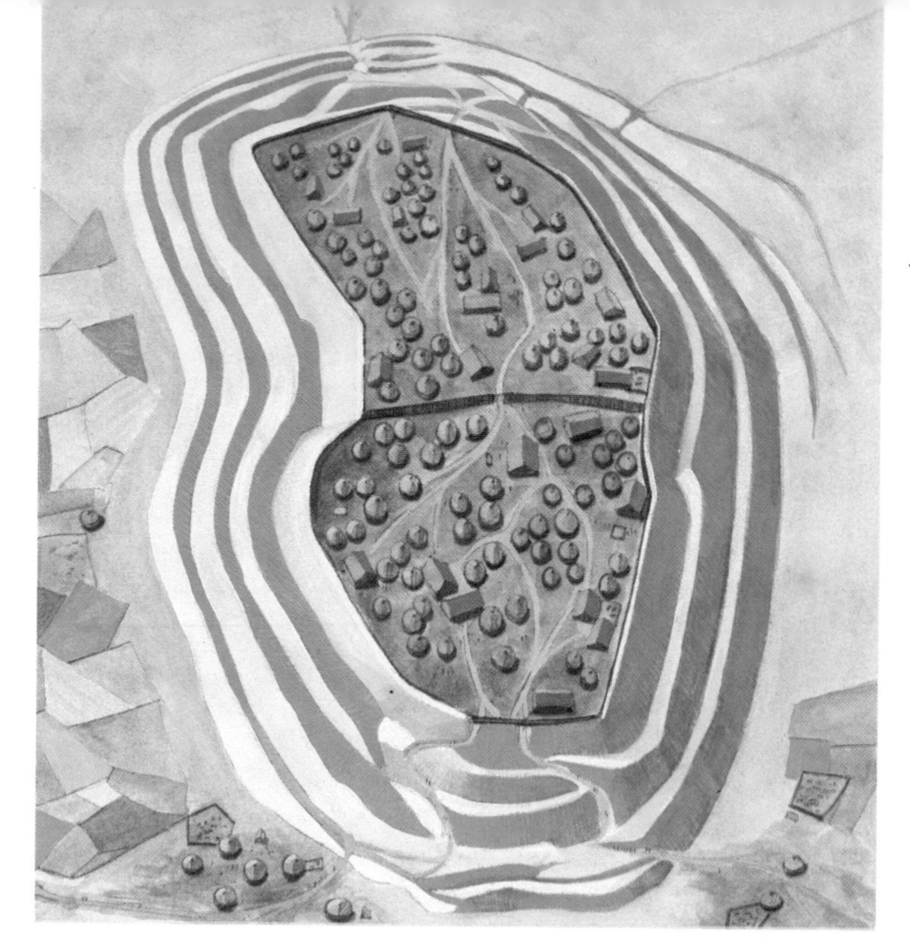

Left *A hillfort was used as the home for the king, his counsellors, warriors and skilled craftsmen, together with their families and servants.*

Other buildings were used as granaries, or places of storage where hay and other important winter supplies could be kept safe and dry. Grain was also stored in large pits dug in the ground and carefully sealed until the contents were needed. Some disused storage pits were used as rubbish tips, while others, enclosed within walls of wattle and daub, acted as communal lavatories.

Cows, pigs and sheep were normally grazed in the fields or open land around the hillfort, although occasionally they were herded inside the ramparts. Some hillforts contained large enclosures where cattle could be penned in. This prevented them from wandering among the huts and houses.

Some settlements also had a shrine or small temple, perhaps placed in an important position just inside the main gates. Here, tribal gods were worshipped and sacrificial offerings made.

Around the hillfort

The Iron Age landscape was dotted with the hamlets, farms and homesteads of families who lived on the plains surrounding the hillforts. These farming settlements lay among acres of small fields and areas of open grassland.

By the time of the Iron Age, the Ancient Britons had cleared large areas of woodland and converted them into fields where crops could be grown or cattle put out to graze. When an area had been cleared, fields would be marked out using stones that had been thrown to the side during ploughing. Known as 'Celtic fields', they were square or rectangular in shape.

Pathways and tracks wound between the fields, linking hamlet and farmstead and leading to the nearest hillfort. These tracks would be used as a supply route, along which cartloads of farm produce could be transported to the hillfort. In return for these goods, the hillfort offered a place of refuge for the farmers and their livestock whenever there was the threat of an attack. However, there was little to prevent a group of raiders from setting fire to their farmsteads, stealing any stray cattle, and murdering those people who had not been able to reach safety in time.

Below *The land surrounding a hillfort was used to grow crops and to graze cattle.*

Lake villages

In flatter areas of the country, where no suitable sites for a hillfort could be found, the Ancient Britons found other ways of defending themselves. In the flat, marshy land of South-West England, for example, and in parts of Scotland and Ireland, they lived in lake villages.

These lake villages were actually floating islands and consisted of a bog floating in the middle of a lake. The inhabitants strengthened the bog with timber, brushwood, stones and clay. A palisade of stakes filled in with wattle and daub was constructed around the perimeter. People travelled to and from dry land in dug-out canoes, which were moored at various landing-stages. On the island, huts were made from wattle and daub and had clay floors and paved entrances. The inhabitants of the village were usually craftsmen, such as metalworkers, potters and weavers. They probably also kept cattle and grew crops in fields on the mainland, as well as taking advantage of the opportunity to fish in the waters around them.

Life in a lake village naturally presented particular problems. Grain could not be stored in pits dug in the ground because the boggy ground was much too wet. Instead, food was stored in huts with raised floors. Constant attention had to be paid to the buildings on the island, as their foundations were continually sinking deeper and deeper into the bog below. This made repeated rebuilding and repairing necessary, with more stones and clay being piled on to the bog.

Left *People living in lake villages used dug-out canoes to get to and from dry land.*

Strongholds and stone towers

In addition to hillforts and lake villages, the Ancient Britons constructed another type of defensive stronghold, called an *oppidum*. These were mostly built in valley bottoms or on low-lying land, and were completely different in design to hillforts. Instead of being surrounded by ramparts, they were defended by a number of dykes — steep earth banks — that were placed on those sides of the *oppidum* that were most open to attack. These defensive dykes were combined, where possible, with natural barriers like rivers and marshes, which further obstructed the passage of any attacking force and its chariots.

Oppida were much larger than hillforts and lake villages. They were like towns and acted as the capital of an area. Because they were often built near rivers or important fords and crossing places, the king was able both to control trade and closely observe those who came and went.

In Scotland, Iron Age Britons lived in round stone towers, called *brochs*. These towers could stand up to 12 m (39 feet) high, and sometimes had a stone stairway linking ground level with the first floor. The ground floor was used as a kind of workshop in which weaving and threshing could be carried out. It also provided shelter for animals during the worst months of winter. The family lived on the top floor because of the extra safety its height might provide in times of danger.

Right *Stone towers, like this one, were built by the Ancient Britons of Scotland. The towers were called* brochs.

4 DAILY LIFE

Iron Age farming

Iron Age Britons ploughed their fields with an ard, a primitive wooden plough pulled along by a pair of oxen. The ard could only scratch small furrows in the earth and was not capable of turning the soil over. This meant that fields had to be ploughed twice, first up and down, then from side to side. Eventually a more efficient plough was developed, equipped with a mould-board that turned the earth over and made proper furrows.

The Ancient Britons grew turnips, cabbages, beans and parsnips. But their main crops were wheat and barley, which they harvested twice a year using small bronze or iron sickles. After the crop had been reaped, cattle could be turned loose into the fields to graze on the stubble and to fertilize the earth in preparation for the next sowing.

Below *Grain crops were harvested using small sickles of bronze or iron.*

Left *The Ancient Britons stored grain in pits in the ground.*

Once transported to the farm, the crops were threshed to remove the grain from the husk. This was done by drying the ears of wheat and barley either in an oven, or by simply setting fire to them, before they were pounded with sticks to remove the husk. The grain was then stored, either in pits or in wooden granaries.

Farmers also kept a variety of livestock, including cows, sheep, pigs and goats. During the spring and summer, these animals would graze in the fields or open pastures. But, because only a small number could be sheltered and fed with hay throughout the winter, the older animals were slaughtered each autumn. Their meat was dried and stored.

The various stages in the farming year were celebrated with religious ceremonies, which were held in thanksgiving to the gods for a plentiful harvest and the health of the livestock. These occasions turned into festivals, at which there was much feasting and drinking. In a good year, food was plentiful, with enough to last through the winter. But a crop failure, or an epidemic among the cattle, could reduce a community to starvation in a few months.

Food and drink

Above *A Celtic stone quern which was used to grind corn into flour.*

Above *Celtic basins of stone.*

Right *At mealtimes large pieces of meat were cut up and eaten with bread, washed down with large quantities of beer.*

The everyday diet of the Ancient Britons consisted principally of corn, wheat and dried meat. The meat of those animals slaughtered during the autumn was preserved by smoking. This was easily accomplished: joints were simply hung up under the roof of the hut and smoke from the hearth quickly cured them. Meat could also be preserved for long periods by salting it, the salt being obtained by mining or even by evaporating seawater.

Cooking could either be performed outside in large troughs, or alternatively indoors upon roasting spits, or in cauldrons that were suspended from the roof.

Hunting provided further sources of meat, particularly deer and wildfowl, but hares or geese were never eaten as they were considered to be sacred animals. For those who lived near rivers, or in lake villages, fishing naturally provided a plentiful source of fresh meat all year round.

Vegetables were cultivated, and, when in season, provided a welcome variation of the daily menu, as did wild fruits and nuts. Corn, once harvested and threshed, was ground to a rough flour on querns: large, flat or slightly bowl-shaped stones. This flour was mixed with water to make a basic dough and then baked in clay ovens. It was also eaten as porridge or a kind of muesli.

The grain of the major crops — barley, rye, oats and wheat — was crushed and fermented to make beer. This was the most popular drink amongst both rich and poor. Great quantities were consumed at mealtimes and this probably encouraged much of the boastful and boorish behaviour for which the Ancient Britons were renowned.

Seated on animal skins spread on the floor, they ate with their hands from low tables. No form of cutlery was used, except perhaps a knife to divide the larger joints of meat. Those rich enough to afford it were able to drink wine, which was imported from Italy at great expense.

Above *Men built hurdles, or fences, to keep cattle from straying.*

Home crafts

Most Iron Age communities were self-supporting. They bought little from passing traders because they rarely needed items made by specialist craftsmen.

Spinning wool and weaving it into lengths of cloth were common domestic tasks, though these were largely reserved for the winter months when the need to work in the fields had slackened. Another frequent task was making cooking pots, jars and bowls from rough clay. These pots were moulded by hand and probably fired in kilns. Generally, every household would make its own pots, decorating them with lines and triangles incised in the wet clay. Later in the Iron Age, potters learnt how to turn pots on a wheel, and this enabled them to make much thinner, finer vessels.

Domestic tools and ornaments were also made in the home. Pieces of bone were carved into combs and ornaments, while the versatility of wood made it a useful material for many implements. Small blocks of wood were

Below *Pottery vessels were often decorated with lines and patterns.*

carved out to make ladles, bowls and cups. Tubs, used for all kinds of storage purposes, were made out of wooden staves held together with supporting bands of iron. The Iron Age handyman also made wooden stoppers and handles for knives, the shafts of spades and sickles, and cut lengths of wood for the construction and repair of walls and roofs. Although farmers were probably capable of making simple carts for general use, the more sturdy and complicated vehicles would have been built by a specialist carpenter.

Basketry and hurdle-making were also everyday crafts. Baskets would have been useful for carrying vegetables back from the fields, and hurdles would have been used to keep cattle from straying.

When iron was first discovered, smelting it was probably also a domestic craft. But full-time blacksmiths soon established themselves as specialized craftsmen, selling ready-smelted lumps or lengths of iron to rural communities. Most farmsteads and hillforts would keep a lump or two of iron in store, and this would be used to make sickles, knives or replacement items for carts and harnesses when required.

Above *This piece of bronze harnessing for a horse was found at Westhall, in Suffolk.*

Below *Spun and dyed wool was woven into lengths of material by the women of the community.*

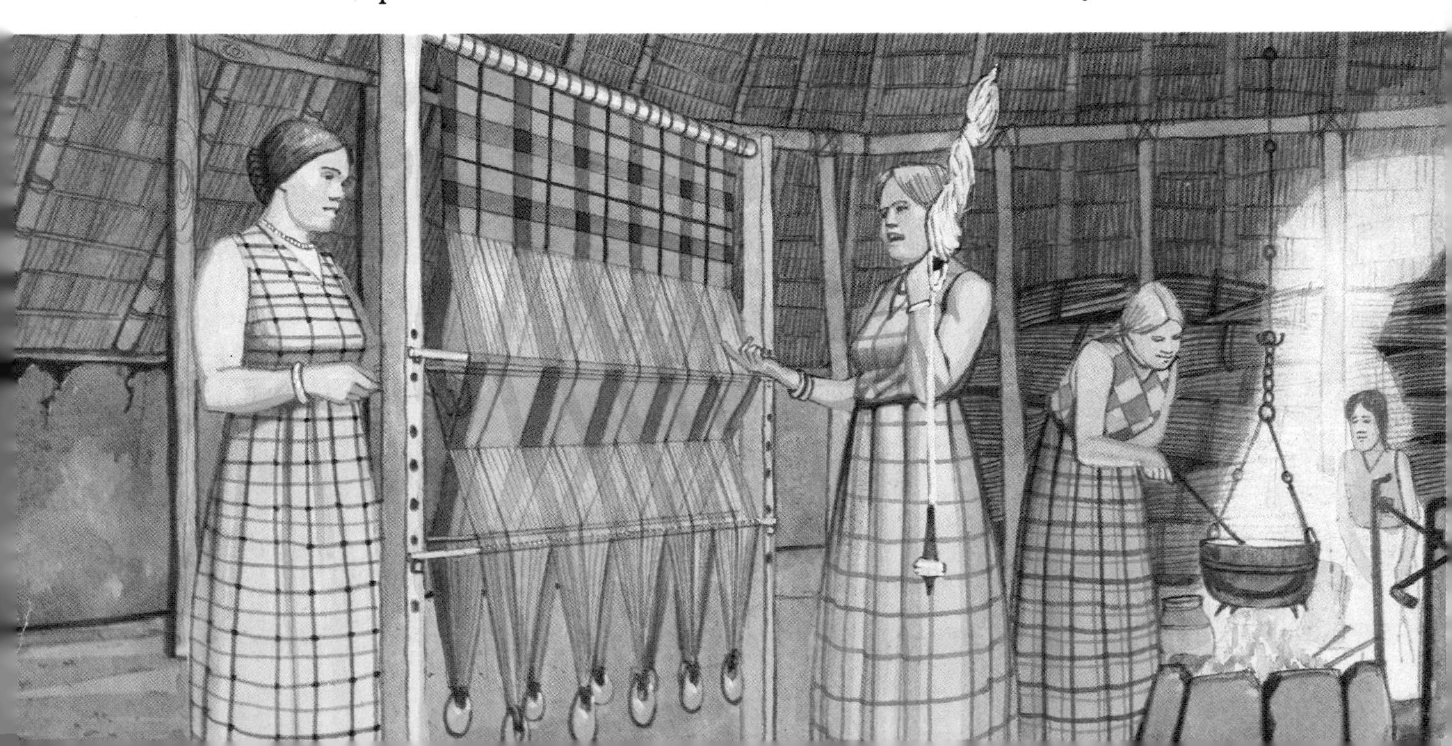

Clothes and jewellery

The Ancient Britons were a handsome race who took great care over their personal appearance. Both the men and the women were especially proud of their hair, which they washed frequently and wore either loose or plaited, sometimes also dressing it with combs and pins. Some

Right *The Ancient Britons took a lot of trouble over their appearance. They liked to wear brightly checked and striped clothes. They also took great care of their hair.*

Left *A necklace of twisted gold, called a torque.*

men wore beards, while others shaved their cheeks. However, nearly all of them let their moustaches grow as long as possible.

The standard items of clothing in the Iron Age were tight trousers and a tunic for men, and long woollen dresses for the women. While animal skins were still used as an upper garment by some Britons, the more civilized among them wore colourful woollen cloaks, thick in winter and thin in summer. These cloaks were woven in bright checks or stripes and could be quite gaudy. Footwear consisted of leather shoes and sandals, or linen shoes with leather soles.

If the Ancient Britons were fond of stylish clothing and jewellery, they also liked to make themselves appear as striking as possible, especially when going into battle. To achieve a terrifying effect, they dyed their bodies with woad, a blue dye obtained from a plant they cultivated for this sole purpose. They also dyed their hair a pale colour and combed it tight over their scalps to reinforce their threatening appearance. The tattoos that they painted over themselves could take the form of scroll patterns, wild animals and imaginary beasts.

Below *The Ancient Britons wore shoes like these.*

5 IRON AGE CRAFTSMEN

The blacksmiths

Blacksmiths, along with other specialist metalworkers, were honoured above all other craftsmen in the Iron Age. As well as providing iron implements for farming and domestic purposes, they were given the prestigious task of equipping the warriors with swords and shields. In addition, they made decorated harnesses for the horses that drew the warriors' chariots into battle.

The Ancient Britons started using iron in about 500 BC. Being a stronger metal than bronze, iron made tougher and more hard-wearing tools and weapons. As a result, farming became more efficient and warfare more deadly. The introduction of iron therefore marked an important step forward.

Iron ore was dug from shallow, open-cast mines. It was smelted in clay-lined furnaces that were fired with charcoal to give greater heat and fanned with great leather bellows. The process of smelting divided the iron ore into a bloom (lump) of pure iron, and slag (cinders and impurities). The bloom was taken out and hammered into shape while it was still hot. Hammering the iron in this fashion, constantly re-heating it to make it pliable, was the only way of shaping the metal at that time. It could not be melted down and poured into a mould because, unlike bronze, iron melts at temperatures far higher than the Iron Age furnaces could achieve.

A blacksmith's tools consisted of tongs, with long handles for holding the red-hot iron at a safe distance, an anvil, a hammer, a file and a poker. With these traditional implements he made simple farm tools like sickles and ploughs. He also made cooking vessels and the tripods

and chains used for hanging them over the fire, spits for roasting and fire dogs for the aristocratic hearth. The blacksmith also produced a variety of weapons, particularly swords and daggers, as well as scabbards. Some of these were further decorated by bronzesmiths.

Some of the iron implements that were produced by the blacksmith were turned to other than practical uses. If the red-hot iron was not needed immediately, the blacksmith would hammer it into sword-shaped ingots. These ingots began to be traded for goods and were used as an early form of money. Because iron was constantly in demand, ingots of it could always be exchanged for other items such as food, clothing or household equipment.

Above *Blacksmiths were vitally important to the Iron Age community because they made farming implements, domestic hardware and swords and shields for the warriors.*

The bronzesmiths and goldsmiths

Above *A Celtic gold bracelet found in Cheshire.*

For over a thousand years, before the discovery and widespread use of iron, everyday tools were made of bronze. However, the coming of the Iron Age meant that bronze gradually became used only for high-class luxuries like jewellery, or as decoration on weapons and harnesses. As a result, the bronzesmiths worked mostly for warriors and other high-ranking people. Gold, the most precious metal, was reserved for the most lavish jewellery. Bronze and gold were both worked in the same way — by melting and casting in moulds. This method allowed complex patterns and designs to be made and further decoration was added by embossing and engraving. Bronze and gold were also inlaid with enamel (obtained by heating lumps of copper oxide) and with precious coral (imported into Britain from the Mediterranean).

The simplest pieces of bronze jewellery were pins, which were worn in the hair, and brooches, used for fastening cloaks and tunics. Thick, cumbersome armlets and anklets were worn by both men and women of high rank. The warriors of the tribe carried decorated scabbards, sword hilts and shields, while their horses were equipped with enamelled harness fittings. Such ornate adornments reflected the valour of the warriors and were proudly displayed in times of war or during rehearsed displays of strength and valour. However, the most beautiful and intricate work produced by the bronzesmith was destined to be offered to the ultimate patrons — the gods. Shields too unwieldy or too delicate to be of use in battle, and spears too beautiful to lose in the hurly-burly of war, were thrown into lakes and rivers as offerings to gods and water spirits. But, though generous to the gods with their bronze, the Ancient Britons did not treat gold so highly. They kept it for themselves. The most splendid

Below *The back of this mirror is a beautiful example of the sort of work done by the bronzesmiths of Ancient Britain.*

artefacts made of gold were torques, heavy neckbands made of twisted strands of gold. These were worn by both sexes and seem to have been made in East Anglia, the territory of the Iceni, Boudicca's tribe.

Below *A customer bargains with the goldsmith over the price of a torque.*

6 RELIGION, SUPERSTITION AND DEATH

The druids

Above *This decorated bronze helmet was not for use in battle. It was found in the Thames near Waterloo Bridge and was probably used in processions, or in religious ceremonies.*

The druids were the official priests of Celtic religion. Only they knew how to conduct its complicated rituals and how to communicate with the gods. The druids also acted as astronomers, philosophers and seers. They were drawn from the ranks of the nobility. Only the king, members of the royal troupe and warriors were of higher rank in Iron Age society. The druids also held political power, giving advice to kings and acting as judges to settle disputes and to decide on rewards and punishments. But the druids' chief role was to communicate with the gods. Dressed in white robes, they officiated at important ceremonies and ensured that every god was honoured with the appropriate form of ritual, asking for help in times of trouble or giving thanks in times of prosperity. Animal or even human sacrifices were offered up on blood-stained altars or thrown into deep pits. When the victim had been killed and the blood flowed freely, the druids would peer anxiously into the entrails for a divine message. This was the moment when a druid believed he came closest to speaking with his god.

The druids and their followers worshipped at shrines and on certain open sites that were considered to be sacred, such as groves of trees, sacred wells and on the banks of rivers. Here water gods received gifts of finely decorated shields and daggers, which were cast into the water by the druids. Humans were also offered in sacrifice, singly or chained together in groups of four or five.

The training of a druid was a long process, as he had to memorize all tribal and religious laws and practices. All knowledge was passed on by word of mouth, as no forms of writing had yet been developed. The arrival of the Romans led to the widespread persecution of the druids, probably because they were central figures in the society of the Ancient Britons. As their numbers diminished, their laws and customs were inevitably lost.

Gods and demons

The Ancient Britons expected much from their gods, who they saw as talented superhumans, supreme in all the skills that they themselves practised and admired. Their gods were therefore master-craftsmen, poets, storytellers, healers, magicians and warriors.

Every tribe had its own god, who was considered to be the tribe's ancestor and father of its king. The tribal god was guardian of law and order, defended the community against disease and disaster, and protected both the livestock and the fields. He was also a warrior-god and was expected to lead his tribe into battle. The goddesses had the role of 'earth mothers', promoters of fertility and fruitfulness in all living things and it was to them in particular that the Ancient Britons gave thanks for good crops and the birth of lambs and calves. They also ruled over the woodland beasts, and in times of war they played a significant role by casting magic spells to increase the chances of victory.

The Ancient Britons also worshipped animals for the powers they were thought to possess. Birds were associated with goodness, healing and purity. Boars, bulls, horses, stags and rams were esteemed for qualities such as strength and valour. The Ancient Britons also believed in the existence of spirits and of a mysterious presence in nature, particularly by waterfalls, streams and rivers, and among trees. Oak trees were thought to hold a special magic and mistletoe was prized as a powerful healer. Omens were sought in even the most ordinary natural events, such as a flock of birds passing overhead or a pair of ducks landing on a lake, and each occurrence was studied for its hidden meaning and divine message.

Religion and superstition filled the daily lives of the Ancient Britons. Although the druids conducted the main ceremonies, everyone had to play a part in paying homage to the gods, for, as well as being powerful and talented superhumans, the gods could be fickle and vengeful.

Right *Ancient Britons believed that rivers and streams had spirits. Here, a gold ornament is thrown into the water as an offering to the river spirit.*

The Otherworld

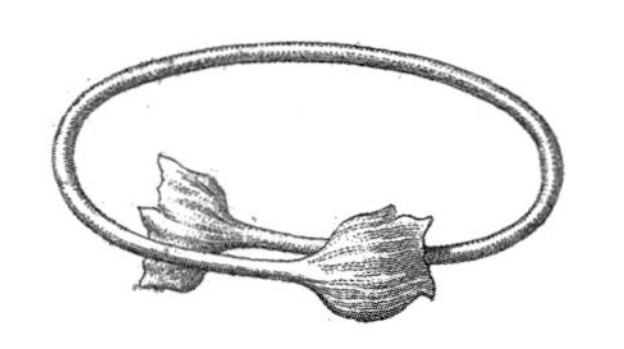

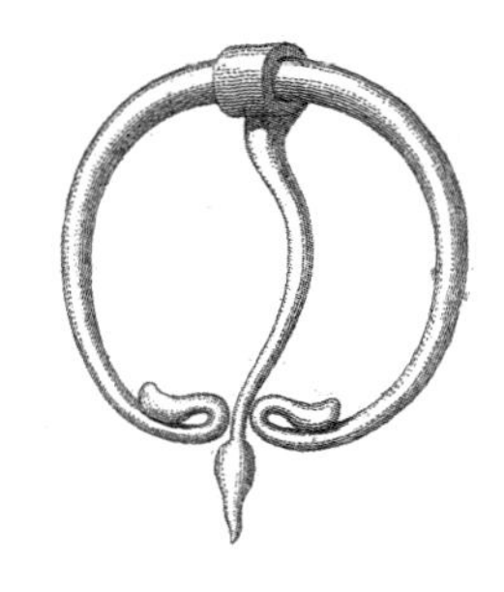

Above *Pieces of jewellery, like this bronze ring and brooch, were often placed in a dead person's grave.*

The Ancient Britons believed that when they died they would go to the Otherworld, the home of the gods and a place of perfect happiness. Everyone went to the Otherworld, whether they had been good or bad in their real lives.

When an Iron Age nobleman died and began his journey to the Otherworld, his body was either cremated and the ashes placed in an urn, or he was buried in a barrow, a grave beneath a great mound of earth. He was equipped with every luxury for his journey after death. In the richest graves would be placed a joint of meat, fire dogs for the hearth and a cauldron for cooking, plates, jars of wine and fine silver cups. There would also be jewellery and ornaments and perhaps a board game to while away the time.

Other noblemen, particularly warriors, went to the Otherworld prepared for action. They were buried with their chariots, a full set of harnesses and sometimes also their horses. Their swords were laid by their sides together with a large supply of spears. However, not everyone could expect such splendid provisions for their burial. Some graves were only furnished with a joint of meat or a simple piece of jewellery. Most people, and especially those who were poor, could expect as few luxuries in death as they had experienced in life.

Left *When an Iron Age nobleman died he was buried with everything he might need for his journey to the Otherworld.*

Feast days

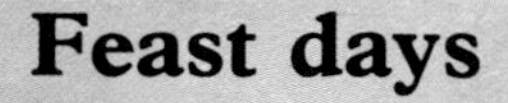

Although the Ancient Britons remained ever watchful that they did nothing to offend the gods, religion in the Iron Age involved a good deal of fun and relaxation as well. Feast days in honour of the gods were held at least four times a year. On these occasions, in addition to religious ceremonies, there would be singing, dancing, and much eating and drinking.

The year was divided into four sections, each marked by a feast. The feast of Samain was celebrated on the eve of 1 November and still survives today as Hallowe'en. It marked the end of summer and the beginning of the Celtic new year. It was considered to be a time of great danger, when the Otherworld became visible, supernatural forces were let loose and the unexpected occurred. This was a night of divination and magic, and sacrifices were offered up to the forces of the Otherworld.

The second feast in the Celtic calendar came on 1 February. This was the feast of Imbolc, sacred to

Brigid, goddess of sheep and other farm animals. The feast of Imbolc ensured the arrival of new-born lambs in springtime, and the ability of the ewes to produce milk for them.

Beltane, the third feast, took place on 1 May. It was another festival connected with farming. Symbolic rites were performed to encourage the growth of crops and the welfare of the farm animals. The druids lit bonfires and the cattle were driven through the flames in order to purify them.

The last feast, Lughnasa, which was held on 1 August, celebrated the harvest of the crops. The festivities and rites surrounding Lughnasa continued for a whole month. This was the last time in the year that country people gathered to enjoy the fruits of their labours, before the weather turned cold and the dark days of winter set in.

Below *During the feast of Beltane the druids drove cattle through the smoke and flames of bonfires in order to purify them.*

7 PEACE AND WAR

The good life

Among the Iron Age nobility, two occupations were loved above all others: war and self-indulgence. When they were not fighting, most noblemen, including the king, enjoyed hunting, games, music, poetry and drinking.

Hunting was considered to be an heroic activity. Birds and deer were hunted for food as well as sport. The boar provided the favourite quarry, as it was the fiercest animal in the forest. Nobles would brag about their strength and skill in the hunt, doubtless exaggerating the size and fierceness of the animal that they had brought down.

Feats of strength and daring were woven into tales and epic poems with which bards entertained the king and his entourage. These tales only encouraged the listeners to try to emulate the achievements of these imaginary heroes when they next went out hunting.

Below *When they were not fighting, the Iron Age nobility liked to relax with plenty of good food and wine whilst a bard entertained them with an epic poem.*

Games were another source of rich entertainment and relaxation. The Ancient Britons played dice, a kind of chess and various other board games. A game resembling hockey was also popular, and imaginary feats on the playing fields also made their way into folk tales and legends.

The lifestyle of the nobility was made more pleasurable and luxurious by the goods that were imported from the Continent. Wine, which was a particular favourite, was brought to Britain from the Mediterranean. It was so highly valued that a jar of it could be exchanged for one slave. These contacts with the Continent influenced some of the practices of the Ancient Britons, particularly the introduction of slaves and the use of money in trading, rather than a simple exchange of goods. However, these new methods of buying and selling were accepted only slowly by the Ancient Britons. As long as the wine flowed and the pleasures continued, such matters made little difference to the luxurious life of the nobles.

To war

The Ancient Britons were an aggressive people. As a Roman historian remarked, 'The whole race . . . is madly fond of war, high-spirited and quick to battle. . .' Unlike the vast majority of the population who were tied to working on the land, the nobles and professional warriors were free to practise their fighting techniques and to rush into

Below *The warriors of Ancient Britain often practised their battle techniques. Their woad tattoos gave them a formidable appearance.*

battle at the slightest opportunity. Hand-to-hand fighting was also popular and quite often occurred during drunken mealtimes. A loud exchange of boasts and insults could quickly lead to a wrestling match. Often men had to be restrained from fighting to the death over a joint of meat.

When involved in more serious disputes, the Ancient Britons usually attacked their enemies in light, two-wheeled chariots that were pulled by a pair of ponies. The sides of the chariot were made from wood or wickerwork, and each wheel had an iron 'tyre'.

Each chariot carried a warrior and his charioteer. Spurring his ponies on with a goad, the charioteer would gallop towards the enemy. When they neared the enemy ranks, the warrior would hurl his spears from the chariot before jumping down and fighting with his sword. His chariot was placed nearby, ready to whisk him away again if the need arose.

8 THE COMING OF ROME

Above *A bust of Julius Caesar who made two unsuccessful attempts to conquer Britain, in 55BC and 54BC.*

The Ancient Britons under attack

The Romans imagined Britain to be on the edge of the world itself, 'at the outermost edge, almost into the whirlpools' and to be separated from Gaul (France) by a channel 'more stormy than any other sea in the world.' Yet this remote country was rumoured to be rich in hunting dogs, timber, slaves, wheat, gold and pearls. The conquest of Britain presented an irresistible challenge.

But the Romans were unable to make a swift conquest of the island. Julius Caesar made two attempts, in 55BC and 54BC, both times meeting with fierce resistance from the Ancient Britons. It was not until AD43 that the Romans, under Claudius, managed to bring Britain firmly under their rule. The Trinovantes could only watch in dismay as Claudius proudly marched into Colchester, their tribal centre, to claim it as his own. One of the fiercest battles took place at Maiden Castle, hillfort and tribal capital of the Durotriges, in Dorset. The tribe's slings and spears proved no match against the Roman onslaught, and Maiden Castle was sacked and the slain defenders buried near the east gate. Meanwhile, the druids, with their secret knowledge, strange rituals and political powers, posed too much of a threat to the Romans. They were pursued and slaughtered, while their religious centre at Anglesey, with its sacred trees, was ransacked.

Boudicca's rebellion, an act of bravery by a conquered people, came just fifteen years later. Although the revolt shook the confidence of the Romans, it did not prevent them from ushering in a new phase in the history of Britain — the end of the Iron Age and the 'Romanization' of the Ancient Britons.

Right *The druids had a hold over the Ancient Britons because of their political and religious power. For this reason they were massacred by the Romans.*

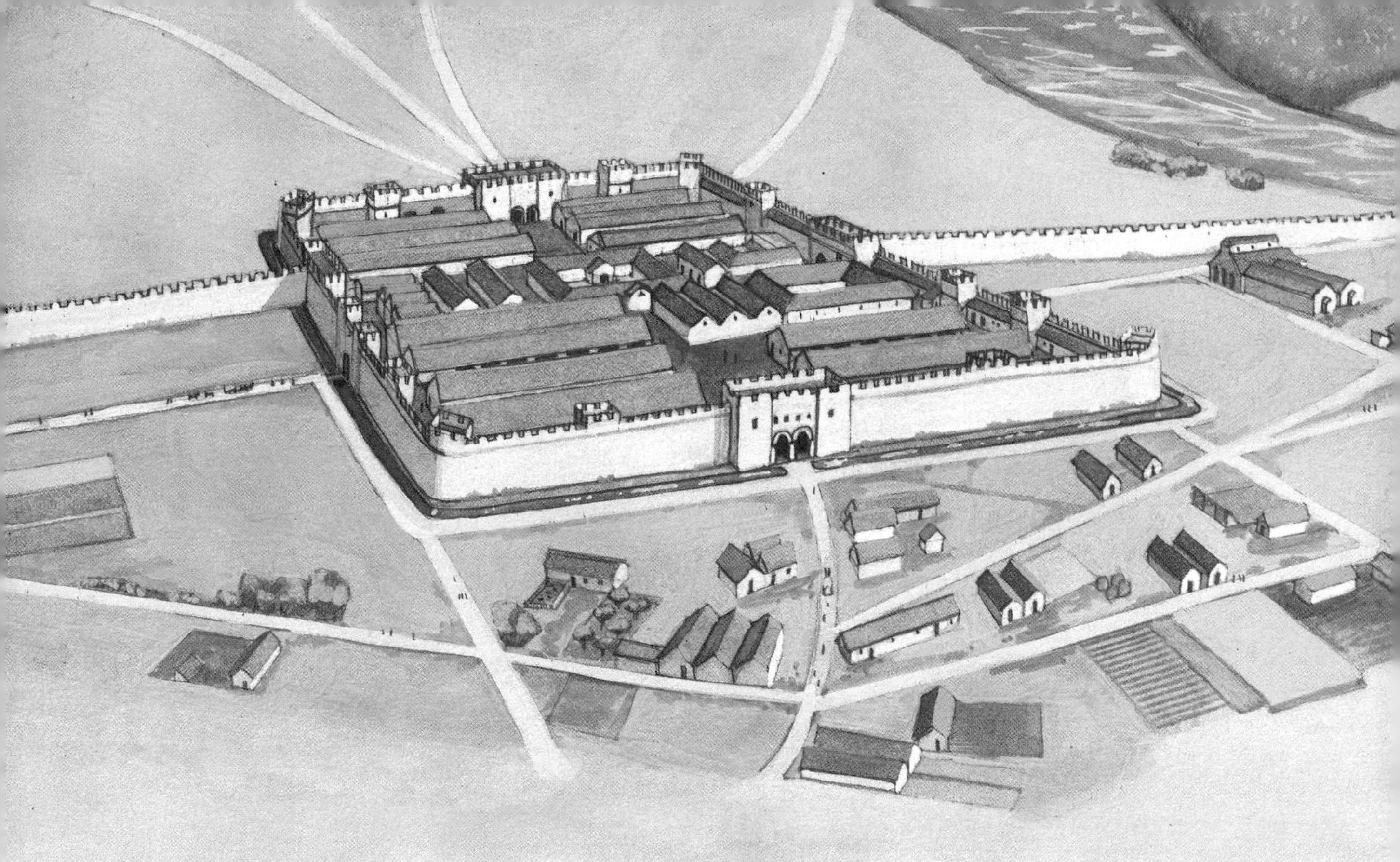

The end of the Iron Age

The Roman conquest heralded the end of the way of life of the Ancient Britons.

The Roman conquest had an immediate effect on the lives of the Ancient Britons. Wars and skirmishes between tribes ceased and Britain, now governed by Roman generals and administrators, entered a period of law and order.

The old tribal systems broke down as the Romans introduced their towns, which now replaced hillforts and strongholds. The Romans built in stone, rather than in wood or wattle and daub. The new towns had markets, temples and other public buildings.

The new towns made the practice of trade and commerce much easier and Britain began to prosper under Roman methods of urban organization. Coins became more common and trade was increasingly conducted with

money, rather than by the exchange of goods. Reading and writing also began to be learnt, at least by the nobility, and some people even started wearing the traditional Roman dress, the toga. It was gradually becoming smart to adopt Roman habits.

But the break with the past was not total. Although the Romans had banned the cruel and bloody religious rites practised by the druids, they allowed the Ancient Britons to continue the worship of their gods. These were now worshipped alongside Roman deities. Some were even combined, as occurred at the temple of Sulis Minerva. This shrine was built by the Romans in honour of Sulis, a Celtic water goddess, and Minerva, a Roman goddess of wisdom.

Elsewhere, on the farmsteads, in the hamlets, and in the remoter corners of Britain, life might not have changed so dramatically. But the Celtic national pride had been destroyed, and the era of the Ancient Britons faded away.

Table of dates

BC

c 8000	At the end of the Ice Age, nomadic hunter-gatherers arrive in Britain.
c 4000 – 3500	Celtic peoples reach Britain from Europe. Farming is established and the first burial mounds and camps are built.
c 2000	More tribes reach Britain from Europe, and the Bronze Age begins. Stonehenge and other ritual monuments (eg Windmill Hill, Silbury Hill, Avebury and Durrington Walls) are built.
c 1500	Bronze Age culture collapses and the camps and stone monuments are abandoned.
c 700	Further influx of Celtic people into Britain from Europe.
c 600 – 400	The first hillforts are built. While some are abandoned, many are made stronger.
c 500	Another wave of Celtic people arrive in Britain from Europe.
c 500 – 450	Beginning of the Iron Age in Britain.
c 75	The Belgae, arriving from France and Germany, conquer areas of South East England and settle there.
55 – 54	Julius Caesar makes two unsuccessful raids on Britain.

AD

43	Claudius successfully invades Britain.
60	Prasutagus, husband of Boudicca and king of the Iceni, dies. Boudicca starts her rebellion and sacks Colchester, St Albans and London.
61	Boudicca leads her army against Suetonius, fails, and poisons herself after the battle.

Glossary

Anklet A piece of jewellery worn round the ankle.

Anvil An iron block on which blacksmiths would hammer metal into shape.

Ard A primitive form of plough.

Aristocracy The upper level of society.

Armlet A piece of jewellery worn round the upper arm.

Barrow A square or round mound of earth built up over a tomb.

Celts An important group of people who lived in Central and Western Europe, some of whose tribes settled in Britain during the Bronze Age.

Cremate To burn a dead body.

Emboss To decorate metal by pressing patterns into it from underneath.

Enamel A glassy, coloured coating used for the decoration of metal.

Engrave To decorate metal by cutting patterns into it.

Fire dogs A pair of iron bars used to support logs of wood in a fire, enabling them to burn more efficiently.

Furnace An enclosed chamber where metal is softened by heating it to a very high temperature.

Granary A store for grain.

Hearth A place where a fire for cooking is lit.

Ingot A lump of metal, usually beaten into an oblong shape.

Iron Age In Britain, the period from about 500 BC, when iron was first used, to the first century AD, when the Romans conquered the country.

Iron ore Iron found in its natural state, mixed with other substances.

Kiln A kind of oven in which pottery is fired to harden it.

Omen A sign predicting a future event.

Palisade A strong, tall wooden fence.

Quern A flat or slightly bowl-shaped stone for grinding grain with a smaller stone.

Ramparts The walls and defences round a hillfort or town.

Ritual A religious ceremony, sometimes involving sacrifices.

Sack To destroy a place or a building by attacking and burning it.

Sacrifice Something or someone killed as an offering to a god.

Seer A priest who predicts future events.

Sickle A tool for harvesting crops like corn, with a small curved metal blade and a wooden handle.

Smelt To separate pure iron from other substances by heating iron ore in a furnace.

Tattoos Patterns and drawings, painted or dyed on to the skin.

Torque A heavy necklace made of twisted strands of metal.

Wattle and daub Twigs and branches (wattle) woven together, then plastered with mud (daub) to form a wall in an Iron Age house.

Woad A blue dye obtained from the leaves of the woad plant.

Further Information

Places to visit

Museums Iron Age objects found by chance, or dug up in excavations, are displayed in most museums throughout Britain. Particularly fine collections are to be seen in London, at the Museum of London and the British Museum. The British Museum also has on display the body of an Iron Age man who was strangled and thrown into a bog about 2,500 years ago and discovered perfectly preserved in 1984.

A full-scale reconstruction of an Iron Age farm can be seen at Avoncroft Open Air Museum, in Worcestershire. You can also see a reconstruction of an Iron Age community at work at Butser Hill, in Hampshire, where experiments in Iron Age farming methods are being carried out near the site of an actual settlement.

Famous Sites South-east England is literally dotted with hillforts. The best sites are Danebury Hill, Hampshire, and Hod Hill and Maiden Castle, both in Dorset.

Celtic fields can also be spotted in parts of south-east England. The most distinctive of these are Fyfield Down, and Smacam Down, Dorset. The Ordnance Survey Map of Iron Age Britain is useful for locating such features.

Books

Cunliffe, Barry *Cradle of England* (BBC, 1972)

Dyer, James *Hillforts of England and Wales* (Shire Archaeology, 1981)

Laing, Lloyd *Celtic Britain* (Routledge and Kegan Paul, 1979)

Ordnance Survey *Southern Britain in the Iron Age* (1962)

Quennell, C.B.H. & M. *Everyday Life in Prehistoric Times* (Batsford, 1959, reprinted 1973)

Ross, Anne *Everyday Life of the Pagan Celts* (Batsford, 1970)

Sellman R.R. *Prehistoric Britain* (Methuen, 1958, reprinted 1970)

Stead, I.M. *Celtic Art* (British Museum Publications, 1985)

Wainwright, Richard *A Guide to the Prehistoric Remains in Britain* (Constable 1978)

Picture acknowledgements

The illustrations in this book were supplied by: The Department of the Environment 18; The Mansell Collection 13, 20 (top), 30 (both), 32, 33, 35 (bottom), 38 (top), 41, 45, 52; The Museum of London 20 (bottom); Philippa Smith 6; The Trustees of the British Museum 14 (both), 35 (top), 38 (bottom).

Index